Dear Vanessa and Andrea Delgado, I hope you can learn Jesus' story through this book! Vanessa, I can hardly wait to have you as my student for next year. God bless you and your whole family!

Love,
Mrs. Heather Cleaver

A CHILDREN'S PLAY OF THE STATIONS OF THE CROSS

AN ADAPTATION FROM THE HOLY BIBLE

Written by Heather Cleaver
Edited by Otilia Nigaglioni

AuthorHouse™
1663 Liberty Drive
Bloomington, IN 47403
www.authorhouse.com
Phone: 1-800-839-8640

© 2011 Heather Cleaver. All rights reserved.

No part of this book may be reproduced, stored in a retrieval system, or transmitted by any means without the written permission of the author.

First published by AuthorHouse 3/11/2011

ISBN: 978-1-4567-3052-9 (e)
ISBN: 978-1-4567-3051-2 (sc)

Library of Congress Control Number: 2011902388

Printed in the United States of America

This book is printed on acid-free paper.

Because of the dynamic nature of the Internet, any web addresses or links contained in this book may have changed since publication and may no longer be valid. The views expressed in this work are solely those of the author and do not necessarily reflect the views of the publisher, and the publisher hereby disclaims any responsibility for them.

PREFACE

I, Heather Cleaver, have been teaching in the Catholic Archdiocese of Chicago for more than ten years, and I wrote the script for ***A Children's Play of the Stations of the Cross*** nearly six years ago for the first and second grade students at my school. I put this into production four times with the help of co-workers. I revised it each time to offer you this masterpiece. I received positive feedback about my play. A parent of one of my students informed me that after having enrolled three children at our school, two of whom had already graduated, this was the best play he had seen at our school thus far. A co-worker had informed me that she needed to step into another room momentarily in the middle of the play because she became teary-eyed over the portrayal of the suffering of Jesus. I thought to myself, I can reach a wider audience and touch the lives of more people if I can make this script available for others to perform. Hence, this play was made into a book for you!

The play is ideally performed by young members ranging from grade levels 1 through 8, and any age group will appreciate watching this touching play. The play runs approximately 20 minutes long, but additional introductions, readings, songs, prayers, meditations, speakers about the subject matter, and final bows/curtsies may lengthen the program by about 5 to 15 minutes (perhaps even longer if scheduled within a Mass or Christian service.)

The Stations of the Cross ties nicely into teaching the Sacrament of the Holy Eucharist in second grade within the Catholic education system, so I supplemented the prayers and teachings in my classroom with the production of my play. Any Christian educator will enjoy reaching out to their school or church community with this prayer service. It may be used by classrooms, school acting groups, or youth groups. Likewise, any theater company wanting to produce this great Christian play can depict the life, suffering, and sacrifice of Jesus to reach out to their communities in preparation of the Easter holiday celebration.

The characters' lines are simple for children to memorize, yet the message they convey hits home to the audience. A minimum of 12 young cast members is required. However, a whole class is able to participate by changing a few things. The size of the angry crowd, weeping women, narrators, optional inclusion of certain characters, and variations in the script may increase the number of your cast members as you see necessary to fill in more roles.

In this book, you will enjoy reading the script for ***A Children's Play of the Stations of the Cross***, personal writing sections, a variety of suggestions on how to present your program to your audience, and blank pages to make your own pictures of the Stations of the Cross. The script includes my very own personal directing notes annotated along the side of the script. These thoughts were stirring in my brain as I wrote and directed the play, but this year, I finally wrote it all down just for you! The play is strong enough to stand on its own as a great program, but you may look at my playbill for supplemental readings and songs. I have provided many suggestions after the script which may satisfy your program's needs. You may want to utilize my suggestions on how to make the props and costumes. If you have your own vision about how the set should look or cool props/costumes that you want to buy or make, try it. Let your creativity soar! I have also included sample letters sent to parents that were used during my very own production (names were deleted).

Read the script several times. Envision this in your mind. If you feel that there is an audience wanting to see this, by all means, put the play together. If this is your first time producing a play, the easy part is done for you. It's already written with many how-to suggestions to help suit your needs! The script is written in larger print for the young actor's ease of reading. The actor's gestures are also embedded within the directing notes along the left side of the script rather than in parentheses and italics so that it does not confuse the very young reader.

If you would like to get more feedback or any other suggestions for your play production, you can e-mail me at mrsheathercleaver@yahoo.com. Let me know how your play turns out. I hope it helps your audience members experience a closer relationship with Jesus. My wish is to help spread the Good News about what Jesus has done for us, and I hope that it does exactly this for your audience and cast members. Have fun with this experience, and God bless you!

This book is dedicated first and foremost to my husband, Andrew Cleaver, who is the love of my life. He has stuck by my side even when I have been a very difficult person to get along with.

Secondly, this book is dedicated to my students—past and present. May they always follow the true teachings of God and grow in their faith each day. They will always remain in my heart.

TABLE OF CONTENTS

SECTION ONE
A List of
The Stations of the Cross
1

SECTION TWO
The Script for
A Children's Play of the Stations of the Cross
An Adaptation from the Holy Bible
*Director's Notes Annotated Along the Side of the Script
*Variations of Script Included
3

SECTION THREE
My Personal Notes
25

SECTION FOUR
Tailoring the Play to Fit Your Needs
*Tweaking the Presentation for a Venue with Muffled Sound and Sound Travel Concerns
*More Tips on Tying Up All the Loose Ends
31

SECTION FIVE
Easy Budget-Friendly Costumes and Props
41

SECTION SIX

Marketing Materials:
*The Playbill
*Sample Letter Requesting Donated Materials
*Sample Letter for Delegated Services
*Sample Invitation Letter

59

SECTION SEVEN

My Pictures of the Stations of the Cross

67

APPRECIATION LETTER

A Note from the Author to the Cast Member

98

I

A LIST OF

THE STATIONS OF THE CROSS

THE STATIONS OF THE CROSS

I	Jesus is Condemned to Death
II	Jesus Takes Up His Cross
III	Jesus Falls the First Time
IV	Jesus Meets His Mother, Mary
V	Simon Helps Jesus Carry His Cross
VI	Veronica Wipes Jesus' Face
VII	Jesus Falls the Second Time
VIII	Jesus Meets the Weeping Women and Children
IX	Jesus Falls the Third Time
X	Jesus is Stripped of His Garments
XI	Jesus is Nailed to the Cross
XII	Jesus Dies on the Cross
XIII	Jesus is Taken Down from the Cross
XIV	Jesus is Laid in the Tomb
XV	Jesus Rises from the Dead

II

THE SCRIPT FOR

A CHILDREN'S PLAY OF THE STATIONS OF THE CROSS

AN ADAPTATION FROM THE HOLY BIBLE

Written by Heather Cleaver
Edited by Otilia Nigaglioni

CAST OF CHARACTERS

Narrators:	1 fluent reader
	(This may be a teacher, student, or parent.)
	You may have about 18 readers, but you may need even more depending if you choose to tailor the script with character readers.
Jesus:	1 boy
Mary:	1 girl
Simon:	1 boy
Veronica:	1 girl
Weeping Women (and children):	2 or more girls
	(You may include additional girls and boys to fill in the roles of children.)
Pontius Pilate:	1 boy
Soldiers:	2 boys (up to 5 boys)
Angry Crowd:	2 children or more
Crucified Man 1:	1 boy (Optional-Refer to script variations found within written text of the play.)
Crucified Man 2:	1 boy (Optional-Refer to script variations found within the written text of the play.)

THE SET

The scene should take place on a stage or in a large room with a front space designed for the majority of the acting. The altar of your church is also an ideal set to serve as the stage. The middle aisle of the room (or a path in the middle of the room marked off with masking tape or other indicators) should be clear so that Jesus may carry the cross along this path up and onto the stage from the back of the room. If the middle of the room is not available, use a side aisle or pathway. It should also be wide enough for both protagonists and antagonists to be lined up along this pathway. Students can sit along the sides of the room on the floor or on chairs, while chairs should be set up along the sides at an angle toward the front for welcomed guests. Narrators will say their lines from a microphone located at the base of the front stage right or other location where a microphone is available. Narrators should sit in a line in the sequence of the script and stand up right before their turn to be ready for their readings.

TWO COMMON ACTING TERMS FOUND WITHIN THE SCRIPT:

Use the following vocabulary words and definitions for your reference. These common terms are used in acting. They are found throughout the annotated notes along the left side of the script.

Stage right: When the actors face toward the audience from the stage, the right side of the stage is called stage right. The right side from the audience's perspective is not considered stage right, as this is turned around from the actor's perspective.

Stage left: When the actors face toward the audience from the stage, the left side of the stage is called stage left. The left side from the audience's perspective is not considered stage left, as this is turned around from the actor's perspective.

THE SCRIPT FOR
A CHILDREN'S PLAY OF THE STATIONS OF THE CROSS
AN ADAPTATION FROM THE HOLY BIBLE
Written by Heather Cleaver
Edited by Otilia Nigaglioni

Jesus stands at the very base of the stage facing the audience standing behind a table with bread and wine. He looks at the whole audience turning His head from one side all the way across to the other side. He picks up the bread and looks at the audience as He says the following lines.

Jesus puts down the bread after lines are read.

Jesus picks up the cup and looks at the audience in the same way.

Jesus puts down the cup after He says his lines.

Narrator:
   The night before Jesus was crucified, He shared His Last Supper with the 12 disciples during the Passover celebration. Jesus offered Himself as the Lamb of God that would take away the sins of the world. As He took the bread, He blessed it and said:

Jesus:
   Take and eat this. This is my body which will be given up for you.

Narrator:
   He also blessed the wine and said:

Jesus:
   Take and drink this. This is my blood.

(There is no need to have an actor portraying Judas, since it is such a small role, and I preferred not to have one of my cast members vilified in such a manner.)

Jesus kneels with praying hands while closing His eyes at the pause.

At the second pause, the soldiers stand on either side of Jesus and place their hands on Him—one on each side of Jesus.

The crowd sits on the floor at the base of the stage at the start of the play. They stand as the soldiers bring Jesus to face them.

Narrator:

After their meal, Judas, one of Jesus' disciples, left to look for the soldiers and guards. He would betray Jesus. He wanted to turn in Jesus and get paid silver coins. He had made a deal earlier with the chief priests to have Jesus arrested (pause). As Jesus prayed in the garden, Judas arrived with the soldiers and guards (pause). He gave Jesus a kiss, which was the signal to the soldiers that this was Jesus, who they wanted arrested.

Narrator:

The soldiers then took Jesus to Caiaphas and the whole Sanhedrin, which were the high priests and the court. They questioned Him through the middle of the night. In the morning, they held a meeting and decided that they would take Him to the governor, whose name was Pontius Pilate, to be crucified.

A Children's Play of the Stations of the Cross

At the pause, soldiers take both arms of Jesus and take Him in front of Pilate on the stage. Pilate is sitting stage left at a diagonal facing the audience.

The crowd moves closer to the base of the stage in a diagonal line/s (depending on the size of the crowd, this will determine how you want the crowd to be viewed in one or more than one line) as Jesus is brought before Pilate.

Pilate stands when Jesus is brought before him by the soldiers.

At the second pause, the crowd uses their pointer fingers toward Jesus with a very sharp punch of one of their arms while showing angry facial expressions.

At the third pause, the soldier uses his whip and raises it high and then onto Jesus, as if striking Him hard. Overemphasis by raising the whip high helps the audience imagine the beatings Jesus suffered.

Narrator:

They accused Jesus about teaching false things (pause). They were jealous and afraid of Jesus, so they made up lies (pause). Pilate questioned Jesus but did not find Him guilty. The crowd brought Him to King Herod, but King Herod told them that Pilate needed to take care of the matter. Pilate still did not want to crucify Jesus, so he had Jesus scourged instead (pause). The soldiers made fun of Jesus by giving Him a crown of thorns and a purple cloak (pause).

On the last pause, one of the soldiers picks up the purple cloak located at the front corner stage left from the start of the play. Both soldiers open it up taking either end and drape it around Jesus' shoulders. One of the soldiers also gives Him His crown, also located front corner stage left. Place it slowly above His head and then pretend to press it into the head.

Jesus winces and shouts as this is done to show agonizing pain.

Jesus:
   Ah!

Narrator:
   Even after the beatings the crowd insisted:

Crowd:

Crowd makes a fist and punches in the air as they say their lines.

   Crucify Him! Crucify Him!

Narrator:

Pilate shakes his head side to side indicating disapproval as if saying no as he faces the crowd.

   Pilate offered to have Jesus released instead of an insane criminal named Barabbas, but the angry crowds chose Barabbas to be released in place of Jesus. They shouted:

A Children's Play of the Stations of the Cross

Crowd makes a fist and punches in the air as they say their lines even louder.

Crowd:

Crucify Him! Crucify Him!

Narrator:

Pilate finally gave in.

Pilate:

I find this man has done nothing wrong. I wash my hands of this. Let His blood be on your hands. Crucify Him if you wish.

Pilate sighs, looks, down, and then faces the crowd as he says his lines, shaking his head side to side. Pilate smacks hands together in opposite chopping motion, and repeats a few times to indicate his disapproval. He points to the crowd as he says: Let His blood be on your hands.

Narrator:

The soldiers gave Jesus a big heavy wooden cross to carry. He was already tired from the whipping of the soldiers, but He took it without complaining.

The protagonists: Mary, Simon, and weeping women should be sitting quietly stage right of the middle aisle along the path with their legs crossed starting from the very beginning of the play. They are spread out in a line in order from the back of the room in sequential order as Jesus comes into contact with each character: Mary, Simon, and group of weeping women. They all stand up when Jesus and the soldiers reach the back of the room.

Jesus and the soldiers cut through right or left side aisle of the room to approach the back in the center of the room, where the cross should be set against a wall. They may have to weave through audience members to get to the back.

The crowd also moves into the middle aisle stage left and stands in a line along the path facing toward the middle (opposite of the protagonists). All characters look at Jesus as He acts out the carrying of the cross.

Soldiers take off the purple cloak, place it on the floor by the wall, and then place the cross slowly and deliberately on Jesus' shoulder.

Jesus leans forward with the cross as if burdened with the heavy weights.

Jesus walks sluggishly and slowly. Then He falls to His knees (He catches himself with one of his hands) and then flat on the floor.

Narrator:

Jesus walked with his cross, but He fell. The soldiers yelled at Him to get up.

A Children's Play of the Stations of the Cross

Soldiers hold onto one side of the cross as Jesus falls, but keep one of the arms of the cross on his shoulder.

Jesus grunts and groans for a few seconds as He lies down on the floor. Jesus counts slowly in his mind to 5 while grunting and groaning.

Soldier counts in his mind to 5 before saying his lines. He yells his lines in angry intonations after Jesus is on the floor for a short moment.

Soldier raises whip and strikes Jesus' back with it (gentle, please).

Jesus gets up and walks a little farther.

Mary cries loudly while covering her face with her hands.

Mary cries a little more before shrieking her lines. As Jesus approaches, Mary reaches out with both of her hands, drops to her knees, and cries out her lines.

Soldier:
 Get up, Jesus! Keep walking.

Narrator:
 Jesus passed by His mother Mary, who was very sad. Jesus was also sad to see His mother's heart break.

Mary:
 My son!

Soldier points to Simon and then to Jesus with the sword.	**Narrator:** 　Jesus was very tired and weak. The soldiers did not want Him to die on the road, because they wanted Him to be crucified, so they pulled Simon from the crowd to help Jesus carry the cross. **Soldier:** 　You there, help this man carry this cross.
Simon has a very sad face.	**Simon:** 　I was just walking by. I have done nothing wrong.
Soldier snarls.	**Soldier:** 　Just do as I say! **Narrator:**
Simon makes eye-contact with Jesus.	But as Simon saw the innocence in Jesus' eyes, he felt sad and horrible for Jesus. **Simon:**
Simon remains in eye-contact with Jesus, and then carries the cross with Jesus by taking the tail end just underneath the arms of the cross as Jesus carries it as well. Both are crouching down and walking sluggishly and slowly.	I will help you carry your cross.

A Children's Play of the Stations of the Cross

Jesus walks to Veronica. Veronica carries a folded felt cloth with Jesus' face already drawn on the inside.

Veronica hands the handkerchief over to Jesus folded with the drawn face concealed as she says her lines.

Jesus opens the cloth just as He is wiping His face. He hands it back to Veronica open and all of the protagonist characters make a gasp in amazement in unison as Veronica reveals the bloody picture of Jesus' face.

Veronica keeps the handkerchief facing outward so that it is revealed to the audience.

Jesus falls with the front of the cross and makes grunting sounds as if in horrible pain for 10 seconds or so. (Count to 10 slowly in your head.) Simon holds onto the opposite arm of the cross so that the one arm lands gently to the ground as Jesus falls.

Narrator:
As Jesus passed by Veronica, one of His friends, she offered a handkerchief to wipe off His blood and sweat.

Veronica:
Take this handkerchief, Jesus. Wipe your face.

Narrator:
His face was imprinted on the cloth as a sign of His appreciation for her kindness. He kept walking, but He was getting weaker and fell a second time (pause).

The narrator pauses before reading his/her lines so that Jesus can grunt and groan for at least 10 seconds. Jesus should get up slowly as if it is very difficult to stand back up.	**Narrator:** Jesus got up and kept walking. He heard many unkind words and many people shouting and laughing.
The crowd should be on the left of the middle aisle as Jesus passes by.	**Crowd 1st Person:** Ha. Ha. Ha. He is so weak.
The crowd points toward Jesus with whole hand with the palm up.	**Crowd 2nd Person:** He thinks He is the Son of God. Let's see how He can get out of this one.
	Narrator:
As Jesus approaches the women, women and children cover their faces and cry.	Jesus came by some kind women and children who were sad. They were crying for Jesus.
	Jesus:
Jesus' eye-contact with the women remains as He speaks to them.	Do not cry for me but for yourselves.
Women face Jesus as they simultaneously say their lines in a sad tone.	**Weeping Women (and children-optional):** We will pray for ourselves and the world for mercy. We want to see God in Heaven.
There should be at least two women assigned. Additional children may be added for more roles and kneel in front of the women.	

A Children's Play of the Stations of the Cross

The narrator should pause to allow Jesus to act out in agonizing pain. Count to 15 in your mind before moving onto the next lines after the pause.

Jesus grunts and groans, staying flat on the ground even longer. Jesus counts to 15 slowly in his head to add to the reflection time for the audience. Slowly, walk up to and climb up the stage as if on Calvary Hill.

Veronica, weeping women, and children follow Jesus and kneel at the base of the stage with praying hands.

Mary walks up and onto front stage right and sits legs crossed on the floor in preparation for Jesus to be laid on her lap.

Soldier unties the knot. He unties one layer and then the next from the double knot on the shoulder. The soldier takes the garment off of Jesus, stares at it, examines it, runs his hands through the cloth, and nods his head up and down slowly as if saying yes with a crooked smile while saying his lines. The other soldier grabs the garment, and both soldiers both tug and pull—like the game, Tug of War.

Narrator:

Shortly after, He fell the last time (pause). He got Himself up, and went to the top of Calvary Hill. The soldiers stripped Him of his garments and placed bets for His clothes.

Soldier 1:

This is a nice garment.

After lines are said, one of the soldiers folds the garment and places it in back corner stage right.

The same soldiers that were along the side of the carrying of the cross or two different soldiers can be assigned to place the bet for Jesus' clothes. If two different soldiers are assigned to nail Jesus' hands and feet, they wait all the way at the back center of the stage from the start of the play with their swords in their hands waiting quietly as the scene unfolds. Simon holds onto the cross upright while the soldier pounds His hands (punch lightly) and then feet to the cross. Simon will remain there until the soldiers take Jesus off of the cross.

Mary (or another assigned cast member) simultaneously pounds on the stage as the soldiers pound his hands and feet to make the sound effect of the nails being driven into Jesus' hands and feet into the cross. Jesus stands in front of the cross.

Soldier 2:
I'll make you a bet for it.

Soldier 1:
Okay, I'll take that bet . . .

Narrator:
Even though Jesus was embarrassed, the soldiers were greedy and wanted His clothes. Then they took Jesus and nailed His hands and feet to the cross.

A Children's Play of the Stations of the Cross

*Optional insertion of lines until the next asterisk.

If you include this portion, two additional crosses need to be set against the wall on the stage from the start of the play.

Additional soldiers may need to be assigned to these roles. Two crucified criminals need to be assigned to these roles if this inserted option is used.

One soldier for each cross holds the crosses as the criminals stand upright in front of the crosses. Soldier(s) take(s) the hands and feet of the two crucified men and pound their hands and their feet.

Mary (or another assigned cast member) simultaneously pounds on the stage as the soldiers pound the criminals' hands and feet. They stand with their crosses both to the right and to the left of Jesus. One soldier can pound both hands and feet of one criminal and then the next criminal instead of two soldiers if actors are limited in number.

*Narrator:

There were two criminals that were being crucified at the same time as Jesus for committing horrible acts against the law (pause). One of the men hanging on the side of Jesus said:

Crucified man turns his head to face Jesus.	**Crucified Man 1:** If you really are the Son of God, why don't you save yourself? **Narrator:** Jesus ignored these taunting comments, and kept praying to His Heavenly Father. The other criminal hanging on the other side miraculously grew a deep faith in Jesus, and said:
Crucified man turns his head to face Jesus.	**Crucified Man 2:** Jesus, remember me when you come into your kingdom. **Narrator:** Jesus replied to the kind thief:
Jesus turns His head to face the apologetic criminal.	**Jesus:** Truly I tell, you, this day, you will be with me in paradise.
*Begin here if previous lines are omitted. Continue if previous lines were inserted.	*****Narrator:** As Jesus hung in agony, he prayed for his enemies. He asked God to forgive the mean people who put Him on the cross.
Jesus looks up as if praying to Heaven, then slowly rolls His head to the left and down as He closes His eyes.	**Jesus:** Father, forgive them; for they know not what they do . . . It is finished.

A Children's Play of the Stations of the Cross

Soldier pierces Jesus' side with the sword. From stage left, strike in between Jesus' back and cross through toward the right side of Jesus to give visual effect of piercing at Jesus' side.

A student turns off the lights in the room. After a few seconds, another faculty member turns the switch on for the spot light on stage.

Soldier kneels, looks at Jesus, and then looks at the crowd to say his lines.

Soldiers take Jesus off the cross and lay him on the ground with His head on Mary's lap (stage front right).

Mary moves rock (originally facing backwards against the back wall behind stage right) in front of Jesus' dead body. She also removes the crown of thorns from Jesus' head and places it next to him.

Narrator:

Jesus died after hanging on the cross for three hours. There was an eclipse of the sun, and darkness came over the sky. The earth trembled, and there was an earthquake. One of the soldiers pierced Jesus' side. Blood and water poured out, and some of the soldiers who witnessed all of this came to believe in Jesus.

Soldier:

Truly, this was the Son of God!

Narrator:

Soldiers took His body off the cross and laid him on Mary's lap. Then, they buried Him in a tomb cut out of rock. The tomb was donated to Mary and the disciples by Joseph, one of Jesus' friends. They laid Jesus' body in the tomb.

If the inserted option in the previous section is used, the crucified men are also taken off the cross by the soldiers to lie in front of their crosses. Soldiers lean their crosses against the wall.

Simon leans Jesus' cross against the back wall of the stage and exits the stage quietly.

After a brief pause for reflection, a student can start the song '*Jesus, Remember Me You When You Come Into Your Kingdom*' – by Taizé. This may be sung a cappella unless a pianist is available. Repeat the song two or three times.

*Pick one of the following endings in the next section. If you would like to depict the resurrection, use Ending Option 1. If you would like to delete the last station, use Ending Option 2. Catholics often delete the last station during The Stations of the Cross prayers to wait for Easter, the actual celebration time of Jesus' resurrection.

A Children's Play of the Stations of the Cross

Closing lines-Ending Option 1:

After a brief pause, assign a cast member, parent, or personnel to turn on all of the lights, and have Jesus rise with both hands stretched toward the audience with his palms facing upwards as a sign of glory and peace. The director may choose to read this last narration very slowly, loudly, and clearly to grab the audience's attention with this message.
Any other closing prayers and songs may be announced at this time. Then, you may let the audience know that this was the end of the play, and have the cast line up on the stage to take a bow/curtsy.

*Refer to the section for *Marketing Materials: The Playbill* for ideas about prayers, songs, and Bible passages to use during the prayer service. The prayers I used are indicated in my sample playbill.

After the end of the prayer service, an announcer introduces each actor along with the role he/she played.

Ending Option 1
*Narrator:

On the third day, Jesus rose from the dead. He overcame death, sin, and won Heaven for all who would choose to follow Him. Let us remember what Jesus has done for us, and let us rejoice for He is living. Let Him live within us.

*Closing Lines-Ending Option 2:
Use this alternate ending if the last station is omitted. The last station is often omitted in prayers in the Catholic tradition, since the celebration of Easter has not yet arrived during the Lenten season. Any other closing prayers and songs may be announced at this time. Then, you may let the audience know that this was the end of the play, and have the cast line up on the stage to take a bow/curtsy.

*Refer to the section for *Marketing Materials: The Playbill* for ideas about prayers, songs, and bible passages to use during the prayer service. The prayers I used are indicated in my sample playbill.

After the end of the prayer service, an announcer introduces each actor along with the role he/she played.

Ending Option 2
*Narrator:

We know that this is not the end of the story. The Devil did not conquer over God's holiness. We await the coming celebration of Jesus' coming—His miraculous resurrection. He overcame death, sin, and won Heaven for all who would choose to follow Him. Let us all remember what Jesus has done for us.

III

MY PERSONAL NOTES

MY PERSONAL NOTES

Here are some suggestions about what to include on the blank lined pages for your own personal acting notes:

- ➢ my role/s

- ➢ page numbers for my character's lines

- ➢ understudy lines

- ➢ director's tips discussed with me

- ➢ start location and movement to different locations throughout the play

- ➢ my lines/acting skills that need more attention and practice

- ➢ pronunciation and intonation of particular words or lines

- ➢ lines I should place more emphasis with a louder or softer volume

- ➢ costumes and props I will use

- ➢ my own thoughts and reflections

A Children's Play of the Stations of the Cross

MY PERSONAL NOTES

MY PERSONAL NOTES

A Children's Play of the Stations of the Cross

MY PERSONAL NOTES

_____
_____
_____
_____
_____
_____
_____
_____
_____
_____
_____
_____
_____
_____
_____
_____
_____
_____
_____

MY PERSONAL NOTES

IV

TAILORING THE PLAY TO FIT YOUR NEEDS

* Tweaking the Presentation for a Venue with Muffled Sound and Sound Travel Concerns

*More Tips on Tying Up All the Loose Ends

TWEAKING THE PRESENTATION FOR A VENUE WITH MUFFLED SOUND AND SOUND TRAVEL CONCERNS

In a big church that has an echo and requires a sound system with speakers for the whole congregation to hear, character voices might not travel well. It may not be feasible for characters to speak loud enough because of the muted effect of a setting with a very large-sized room and a high ceiling. The echo may cause an indiscernible message or misinterpreted speech. If these are concerns you may have, test out your area of interest for the set by checking for its sound quality. You may have to use an alternate approach in the format of the play.

You may want to ask personnel if there are wireless microphones available for your actors' use. If only one is available, you may have to be creative and have actors pass it along from one character to the next, as the play unfolds.

If this is something that is absolutely unattainable, assign more people the roles of reading characters' lines, so that they can speak into a microphone and read the lines while the actors silently act out the parts with emphasized facial expressions. Of course, you will have to assign more roles, but you can be creative by assigning readers more than one role.

I was very fortunate with my room choice. The actor's were able to speak loud enough for audience members to hear their voices without the use of microphones. The ceilings were low, so an echo was not a concern of mine. In the future, I may put the production in a church setting, which may have a very high ceiling. Therefore, I may choose the route of having readers speak the lines into the microphone as others silently act out the characters' parts.

MORE TIPS ON TYING UP ALL THE LOOSE ENDS

This section is meant for the directors and producers of the play. In the following pages of this section, I offer many suggestions for you to bring your ideas together for tailoring the play to fit your needs. You do not have to incorporate all of these ideas into your program. These are merely suggestions. Pick the ones that will work for you and your program. This useful information will help if you are new to the theater, and you may utilize these pages as your checklist. Think about the setting, the target audience, the resources available, and your overall goals when planning your program. Use these notes, and check off or highlight the suggestions that sound feasible. Write your own notes along the left margin to brainstorm your ideas.

__**Pick a venue** for the performance and check its sound quality.

__**Discuss your expectations** with actors and communicate your thoughts and ideas about the play with them often.

__**Emphasize** to narrators and characters that they need to speak **slowly, loudly, and clearly!** Repeat this several times during your practices if you have to!

__**Read the play aloud** with the children one or two times before you assign parts.

__**Cross out the script's lines that you will not use** in both the director's and all of the actors' copies. There are optional insertions and different closing lines that you may choose in the script.

__**Send home the play** for actors to read and practice the script. **Then, have auditions**.

__**Pick their parts**, but remind members that roles are not set in stone until they can feel comfortable with their jobs.

__**Assign narrators and soldiers their numbers** and write the numbers directly into the script. Indicate these both within the director's notes and within all of the actors' books.

__Highlight their characters' parts, and **send** it home with them to **practice for homework**.

__**Assign understudies**. This is just to cover absences due to family emergencies, illnesses, or other such causes. For instance, if you have a large crowd, have one crowd member practice to be a soldier and memorize each soldier's lines. If you have several narrators, have your best narrator practice all of the narrations in case one does not show up. You may even have one of your first narrators be the understudy of characters seen later in the play. You can highlight the understudy parts in a different colored marker to differentiate their part and their understudy part.

__**Mark off with a red vertical line where** you would like readers and actors **to pause** within the text. These pauses can be used as cues to let the actors know that they should finish their gestures. If you would like narrators to wait before reading so that the actor may finish their gestures, mark a read vertical line right before his lines.

___**Discuss with actors that they are responsible** for taking care of their own props and that they may include notes in their personal notes section about what expectations you have regarding these.

___**Explain** to actors where their **start location is and how their movement** throughout the play **changes** within the set. You may want to put an X with masking tape or color coded stickers to show actors where to stand. This might not be feasible in a church, but you may want to use pew numbers and other items within the church to cue the students in on where to stand. Fortunately, we had pillars in our auditorium along with some colored tiles on the floor. I used these to indicate where actors should stand.

___**Practice, practice, practice!** Start 3-4 weeks before you put the event on. If songs are part of your prayer service, teach the actors those as well. Allot practice time for singing if this is part of your prayer service as well. The last week prior to the play, practice your play 2 times everyday. Your final two practices should be dress rehearsals and a run through of the whole program, including singing rehearsals. This will allow the actors to get a feel for their costumes instead of playing with them on the day of the program. This will also allow them to have a chance to practice manipulating their props in the correct manner, such as untying Jesus' garments, pointing the swords, etc.

___**Discuss music** options with a pianist or other musician.

If you decide to sing a cappella, then you might skip this step all together. One year, I asked the music teacher to record her playing one of the songs on the piano, so we sang along to the tape. Other years, I taught my students the songs, and we sang a cappella.

___**Discuss your program with a pastor** for more ideas about readings or other prayers to include. You may tailor your program for your own personal messages that you really want to emphasize. If you would like to use my program, refer to the playbill that I used (See section on ***Marketing Material: The Playbill***).

___**Make props and costumes** (See section on ***Easy Budget-Friendly Costumes and Props***).

___**Make a background scene**. If the set is the church altar, you may not want to make any special background scenes. You may decide to make a little hill against the sky with green and blue bulletin paper taped against the back center wall. During our last production, we had a St. Baldrick's banner in the background of center stage, since the play was paired with our charity fundraising event, so we didn't make a background scene.

___**Pair your program with another charity** or **community fundraising event**. I have to admit, the charity event was not my idea, but I collaborated with many co-workers and decided to pair the prayer service and charity events together. The idea was genius!

___**Charge** a set **admission OR** recommend an **open**

contribution so that you can give your proceeds to charity (See section on ***Marketing Materials: Sample Invitation Letter to Attend the Play***) or your community's needs. My school community had students participate by fundraising for the St. Baldrick's Charity for cancer research on children. Many boys received money from sponsors for St. Baldrick's, and they shaved the hair off of their heads to raise cancer awareness. Additionally, many students participated by cutting their hair and donating it to Locks of Love, a company that makes wigs for children who have cancer. We had asked hair stylists from our community support for their volunteer service to cut hair for those who wanted to donate it and to shave the heads for those raising money for St. Baldrick's. This event was scheduled right after the play. I cut over 10 inches of my hair for Locks of Love. Refreshments and pizza were served during this time, which was a great time for audience members to socialize. This was a great event that further sent out the message of giving and sacrifice, a nice conclusion to our prayer service.

___ Have the **admission fees pay for the costumes and props** you spent, and the rest can all be given to your choice of charity institution or community's funds.

___**Delegate services!** Besides cast members, you may want to choose a team to collect admissions at the door, volunteers to help create your props, and/or technology support to attach information regarding your program's information to your website. I sent a letter to the teachers at my school to pass out the playbill to the students (See section on ***Marketing Materials: Sample Letter for Delegated Services***). I also had one of the teachers pass these out to the audience members. The last year I produced the play, they were placed on the table at the door, and one of our staff members collected admission fees (admission fees were recommended for the charity but not required).

___**Brain-storm** ideas **and collaborate** with co-workers and cast members. This is how we came up with the idea to raise money for a charity and pair it with the program.

___**Schedule communal time** for your audience members. Refreshments following the play allow time for your audience members to share their thoughts and reflections about Jesus' story.

___**Make a playbill**. (See the section on ***Marketing Materials: The Playbill***). I didn't do this for my first production, but I think that this added a nicety for the audience and relatives of cast members. This provision of a playbill will serve as a special keepsake for cast members and relatives. I had the teachers pass them out to the students and audience members. The last year of my production, it was placed on the admission table by the entrance door.

___**Write letters** requesting donated materials or ask co-workers or community members **for some of the needed materials**. People you know are most likely willing to let you have/borrow these items for your production. Many probably have these items lying around somewhere in their household. In my letter to parents, I asked for white bed sheets, but you may also want to request brown pipe cleaners, pillow cases, and their time of service to create props. (See section on ***Marketing Materials: Sample Letter for Requesting Donated Materials***).

___**Send out an invitation.** As previously mentioned, you

may want to suggest donations for admission and give it to a charity. Perhaps you want to give the money for something your community needs, like fresh paint for a room, fixing a leak, or setting up a meal service for couples who just had a newborn. Include all of this information in your invitation. This might help the attendance of your play if audience members know that it supports a good cause. Read the section on **Marketing Materials** to view a sample invitation letter to attend the play.

V

EASY BUDGET-FRIENDLY COSTUMES AND PROPS

EASY BUDGET-FRIENDLY COSTUMES AND PROPS

The actors' lines and narrators' readings tell the story of Jesus' Passion. However, costumes and props definitely add visual appeal to the play. The following costumes and props within this section were used in my play, with the exception of a couple of items: Pilate's clothes and the crucified men's crosses. I did not use the optional insertion of script with the crucified men, so I didn't need two extra crosses. Pilate's headpiece sufficed to distinguish Pilate from the other characters. If there are no costumes or props indicated for a particular character, the actors wore their regular school uniform, but you may want your actors to dress in a particular uniform color scheme or nice clothes. You don't need to use all of the costumes and props listed. They are optional, so pick the items that are attainable with your resources and within your budget. If you have more ideas, use them! The possibilities are endless.

Most of the materials only cost a few dollars except for the bed sheets and pillow cases, so you may buy them if this is within your budget. However, many of the people you know most likely have the items necessary for costumes and props in their household if you don't already have them yourself, and they are most likely willing to donate these items for your use. Consider asking around for some of the common items, such as electrical tape, a saw, aluminum foil, rulers, pillow cases, and bed sheets. Your co-workers, friends, and families of cast members are all very useful resources.

The costumes and props I used hardly cost me a thing because I utilized a lot of resources that were available to me. I asked the parents of my cast members to donate white bed sheets and a blue bed sheet (Refer to section on **Marketing Materials: Sample Letter Requesting Donated Materials**). You may want to ask for these and other items in your letter, such as dark brown pipe cleaners, silk floral arrangements, electrical tape, etc. I made all of the costumes and props myself (except the cross), but you may want to ask some volunteers for service in creating your props. You can schedule a get-together for people to help you. Perhaps even the maintenance workers can help. This may especially be helpful if you are feeling overwhelmed.

I was fortunate to have many of the items I needed on hand. I had electrical tape, aluminum foil, silk floral arrangements, wood glue, wood filler, and tools within my own household. Common classroom items, such as rulers, geometric shapes, and pipe cleaners were also some supplies I already had at my school. I used my own pillow cases, but white bed sheets and one blue bed sheet were lent to our actors by parents. The only items I had to purchase were the purple remnant cloth, the wood for the cross, and the hardware for the cross. These items cost me under ten dollars all together. I was also very lucky to have a handy husband. He made the cross for my play, and he was kind enough to provide me with the steps so that I could share it with you. The creation of my props and costumes was one of the most fun experiences in the production of my play, so have fun creating them!

> **Narrators' clothes:** All narrators may wear their school uniforms, nice clothes, or all one uniform color for shirts and one uniform color for slacks. One year, I gave each narrator a necklace made from a string of fancy thread and sewed it into a foam cross about 2 ½ inches long as the charm.

> **Jesus' wooden cross:** You may choose from two different sets of directions. If you use option 1, you will need a power drill with a 3/8" bit, a saw, a permanent marker, a 2"X 3"X 8" piece of pine wood (perhaps 2 pieces depending on the height of the actor who is cast as Jesus), 60 grit sandpaper, 3/8" diameter dowels that are 2" long, and wood glue. If you use option 2,

you will need a 2"X3"X8" piece of pine wood, a saw, a pencil, 2 bolts that are 4 ¼" in length, a drill bit to match the size of the bolt's diameter, 2 matching sized nuts to fit over the bolts, and a ratchet. The following measurements were used for a boy approximately 3'10" tall. Depending on the height of the character, you will need to lengthen or shorten the pieces of wood. Make sure that the longest piece is a couple of inches taller than the actor who plays Jesus. If option 1 is used, you will need to add a 1/2" to both of the shorter pieces (for the arms) for every inch that you add to the tallest piece of wood. If option 2 is used, add the same amount of inches for both pieces of wood to remain proportionate.

➢ **Option 1:** Cut a 4' piece of wood and two 15" pieces of wood with a saw. The 4' piece of wood will stand vertically. On the 4' piece of wood, measure 1' from the top end and mark with a marker on both 2" sides. This is where the arms of the cross will be positioned horizontally. On the end of the 15" piece of wood, you will need to drill two holes 1" long into the wood approximately 1 ½" apart from each other. Place a moderate amount of glue into the two holes. With a hammer, tap in the 2" dowels into the holes halfway so that 1" is in the hole and the other 1" sticks out. Remove excess glue with a paper towel. Repeat these steps on the other 15" piece of wood. Allow thirty-five minutes to set and dry. With a marker, color the ends of the dowels and align with the marking on the 4' piece of wood so that the arms are 1' from the top of the cross. The markings left from the dowels will be where you will place glue in the hole and place the 15" piece of wood. Fill in the seams with wood filler. Allow the cross to dry 2 days. Sand the finished cross by hand or with a sander after 2 days.

A Children's Play of the Stations of the Cross

This is Jesus' wooden cross Option 1. The cross is one of my favorite props, but I have to admit, it was not made by me. My husband completed all of the woodwork for me. He had to make the dimensions small for one of my very young actors, but you may need to make this prop shorter or longer depending on the height of the actor who will portray Jesus.

Option 2: Cut the wood into a 4' length piece of wood and a 3'3" length piece of wood. On the 4' piece of wood, measure 1' down from the top and mark the wood with a pencil for the intersection. Place the 3'3" piece of wood in the center and intersect with the 4' piece of wood perpendicularly on the flat 3" sides. Drill 2 holes approximately 1 ½ inches apart all the way through both pieces of wood at the intersection. Screw in the bolts and tighten the nuts on the ends of the bolts with a ratchet. This variation is similar to the two types of swords given (Refer to the **Soldier's sword** instructions later in this section). Instead of being flat, this will overlap at the intersection. This is a little easier to make, so I would have used this option if I were to make it myself, since I'm not so handy with tools. Sand the finished cross by hand or with a sander.

- **Two crucified men's crosses:** Use the steps for Jesus' cross to make two replicas if you are going to use the full length script with the optional insertion. (Refer to **The Script for *A Children's Play of the Stations of the Cross*** section.)

- **Jesus' garments:** You will need one white bed sheet or tablecloth. Fold it in half lengthwise if it passes the actor's feet. The actor should wear a white T-shirt and dark shorts underneath. This will be exposed during the stripping of Jesus' garments. Keep one corner of the bed sheet on top of the right shoulder; and wrap the longer side across the back and around to the front. Continue wrapping across the chest. Tie the top two corners of the sheet in a double knot over the right shoulder. Make sure the knot is not tied too tightly so that the soldier is able to take it apart.

A Children's Play of the Stations of the Cross

The bears are shown using pillow cases folded in half lengthwise instead of a table cloth or bed sheet to accommodate for the smaller proportions. They are not wearing a T-shirt or shorts, so this gives a clear picture of what Jesus' garments should look like. The first bear is shown with the corner of a pillow case over the right shoulder with the longer side wrapped around the back and then across the front. The second bear shows the garment with the two top corners of the cloth knotted by the right shoulder.

> ➢ **Jesus' crown of thorns:** Use approximately 10-15 brown pipe cleaners. Weave together to make a crown of thorns. Make it very rugged, and have the ends point outward so that it doesn't poke into the child's head. Use the following steps and pictures to have a clearer understanding.

The finished crown of thorns is shown here from the side view. This is my pride and joy. The crown of thorns is also one of my favorite props that I created for this play.

Step 1:
Using 2 pipe cleaners, double twist them together so that they intersect, and repeat several times leaving approximately 1-2 inches between every intersection. Pipe cleaners are very flexible and easy to work with, so the loops created in between can be bent into corners or left rounded. Leave about one inch ends for each pipe cleaner to stick out as poky thorns.

Step 2:
Attach pipe cleaners to loose ends and repeat step 1.

A Children's Play of the Stations of the Cross

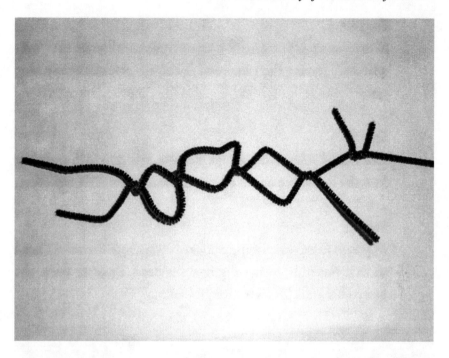

Two pipe cleaners are twisted to form intersections, and the third pipe cleaner is attached to the end. Use this third pipe cleaner to attach another one, and repeat step 1. Then, use step 5 to harness and reinforce the headpiece for a smoother transition from pipe cleaner to pipe cleaner.

Step 3:

Form your piece into a circle to make the headpiece. Fit it to your own head to estimate the size, but it may need to be a little smaller depending on the size of the actor's head. Alternatively, fit it right onto the young actor's head. Make it loose enough so that it doesn't feel tight and give the actor a headache. However, make sure it's not too large that it falls onto the actor's eyes. Pipe cleaners are very flexible, so if it's too large, bend some of the spaces in between to tighten the headpiece.

Step 4:
Weave more pipe cleaners over or underneath your first layer while still leaving the 1 inch end from each pipe cleaner sticking out.

Step 5:
Cut 1 ½ - 2 inch pieces of pipe cleaners, fold it in half, and twist into the headpiece one at a time to create a more thorny effect.

Step 6:
Move all loose ends facing outward away from the actor's head so that the ends do not dig into his head. Bend or curve the protruded ends for a very rough look.

This is the finished crown of thorns from the top view. All of the ends point outward away from the actor's head.

> **Jesus' purple cloak:** Purchase a purple remnant from a fabric store that is big enough to wrap around both arms. Approximately 48" X 60", much like the high priests' outfits. It will be wrapped around without a safety pin.

> **High priests' garments (the angry crowd):**

Option 1: Use one white bed sheet and one safety pin per character. Wear a white T-shirt and dark slacks or school uniforms underneath the bed sheets. Drape the ends of the bed sheet around shoulders and arms from back and neck, and then clasp together in the front with a safety pin. Spread the bed sheet out along both sides of arms until it reaches the wrists, and keep it loose around the back. Remember, it's for a male high priest garment; it's not a scarf scrunched high around the neck nor is it a tight evening wrap for an evening gown! The garments remind me of a bathrobe—only without the actual holes for the sleeves and without the bathrobe belted tie. If these are borrowed materials, indicate their owners by labeling their names on masking tape affixed to the inside of the garment. You could use the safety pin with a label attached as an alternative, but then you have to remember to keep the right safety pin with the matching garment when you store it. Labeling the sheets will make it easier for you to return the materials to their rightful owners after your program.

Option 2: Use altar servers' white garments. Use one per character as an alternative if you are able to get permission from the church to borrow them.

> **Mary's clothes:** Drape one blue bed sheet from the top of Mary's head down her back with the sides draped around her

arms. Fasten the bed sheet to the top of Mary's head and along the sides of her head with 4 bobby pins. Safety pin the two sides of the bed sheet in the front just underneath her neck. Mary may wear her school uniform or nice clothes under the bed sheet.

➢ **Veronica's handkerchief:** approximately 11" X 11" white or light colored felt cloth. Draw Jesus face with crown of thorns and blood with permanent markers. Veronica folds this in half to conceal Jesus' face until he opens this up to wipe His face.

I drew Jesus' face on white felt cloth using a black marker for Jesus' face, hair, mustache, and beard. I used brown marker for his crown and a red marker for small specks of blood.

➢ **Veronica's and Weeping women's headpieces:** Use a solid-colored pillow case fastened to the head with 2 or more bobby pins for each character. Pin the bobby pins higher up on the side of the head as pillow cases tend to fall back off the head. Do not use blue, since that is Mary's color. Veronica and the weeping women may wear their school uniforms or nice clothes with their headpieces.

➢ **Cup of wine and bread:** A wooden cup or a chalice from church can be used to represent the cup of wine. A drawing of bread or real French bread on a plate should also be placed on the table.

➢ **Table for last supper:** Use a student desk without a chair attached. A white tablecloth or bed sheet over it is optional.

➢ **Soldier's sword:** You may need more than one sword, but not every soldier needs one. One of the other soldiers may have a whip. I used the small-sized sword for a second grader. It is the ideal size for a younger cast member, but either size will suffice for the actor, regardless of size or age. I suggest you utilize the materials you have available. Here are two ways to make one.

Small-sized sword: Place two 1-inch squares (geometric shapes used by teachers) next to a flat wooden ruler approximately 1-inch wide. Set the one square on the left side and one on the right side about 4 inches up from the bottom of the ruler. For the sword handle, wrap black electrical tape across and in the back spiraling upward. Start the tape from the bottom of the ruler, up the handle, and then horizontally across the left square, ruler, and right square until the handle portion is completely covered. Keep the pieces tightly next to each other, so the pieces don't move within the tape. To make the blade, tape one equilateral triangle with a 1-inch side (geometric shape) to the tip of the ruler. Tape both the front and back sides of the seam to bind the pieces tightly together. Wrap aluminum foil around the rest of the ruler and triangle portion to make the blade portion of the sword. A picture of this version is shown.

This is the small-sized version of the sword. The foot long wooden ruler, the geometric shapes, the aluminum foil, and electrical tape are used to build this sword, as shown first. The finished sword is shown underneath the required materials.

Large-sized sword: Make the sword out of a wooden yard/meter stick and a foot long ruler, and an equilateral triangle with a 1-inch side. If you do not have the geometric shape, then fold aluminum foil several times, and cut through all the layers into an equilateral triangle with a 1-inch side since this will be used as the tip of the sword. This will look a little different from the smaller sword, because you overlap the 12 inch ruler with the larger ruler about 6 inches up from the bottom of the longer ruler to form a perpendicular intersection. Wrap the two rulers a few times together with black electrical tape to form an X at the intersection. Cut the tape, and then start wrapping the electrical tape from the bottom of the ruler spiraling upward toward the intersection. Continue wrapping over and around the intersection, and then wrap the arm of the sword to the end with the tape. Cut the tape, and wrap the tape starting from the other end toward the intersection. Reinforce the intersection with more electrical tape with the X pattern as many times as needed. Refer to the smaller-sized sword version to make the blade portion of the sword. If it's easier for you to buy a toy sword, then you may check out if any costume places have them.

- **Soldier's whip:** Use a dowel approximately 8 inches in length. Using a skein of dark-colored yarn (black or dark brown), start with one end and wrap it around the entire dowel spiraling down to the other end, tuck in both loose ends. You may need to glue the ends down if they don't stay tucked in. Attach pipe black or dark brown pipe cleaners inside the yarn about one inch deep toward one end of the dowel. Attach them by tucking them into the yarn, and wrap more of the yarn around the pipe cleaners. Glue it down, and reinforce by wrapping more yarn. Attach aluminum crinkled up into balls at the exposed ends of the pipe cleaner to create the spikes at the end of the whip.

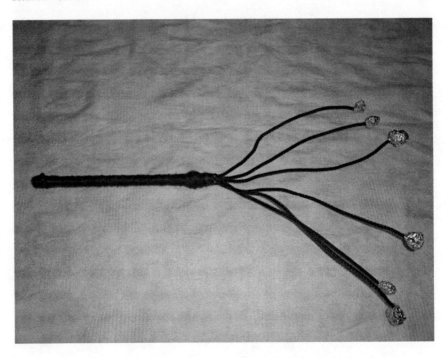

The dowel is wrapped with yarn, and several pipe cleaners are inserted at one end. The exposed ends have aluminum balls at the tips for the spikes.

> **Pilate's clothes:** Use one white bed sheet. Make the outfit just like the high priests, but belt it at the waist with a black one inch tie (like a bathrobe tie, karate belt, or other belt).

> **Pilate's headpiece:** Use pipe cleaners to form a circle fitted around the actor's head. Twist the ends flat against each other so that the ends do not poke out. Affix silk leaves and sprigs to the circle using green or brown pipe cleaners or twist wires (like those found on the packages of bread) found at a craft store. Conceal the ends by pressing them flat against the circular pipe cleaner or hiding it behind the silk foliage. Do not use the flower portion of the silk leaves unless it is small like baby's breath.

A Children's Play of the Stations of the Cross

Pilate's headpiece is formed into a circle using two pipe cleaners as shown on the left side of the picture. The right side of the picture shows Pilate's finished headpiece with the silk foliage twisted onto it with short pipe cleaner pieces.

> ➤ **Rock:** Draw a rock on a large poster board and tape or glue it to the empty cardboard box. I used two emptied boxes from copy paper reams, and I stapled the boxes together. It was easy for the young actor to move this prop since it was so light. The rock will protrude beyond the box, since it will cover a big portion of Jesus' body during the burial.

VI

MARKETING MATERIALS:
*The Playbill

*Sample Letter Requesting Donated Materials

*Sample Letter for Delegated Services

*Sample Invitation Letter

MARKETING MATERIALS

In this section, I have included the playbill, a sample letter requesting donated materials, a sample letter for delegated services, and a sample invitation letter. Refer to the section on ***Tailoring the Play to Fit Your Needs: More Tips on Tying Up All the Loose Ends*** to find out how to utilize the playbill and these letters with your program. Again, these are all different options that you may or may not wish to incorporate. I have presented you with the materials I used in this section as an extra reference. I used these letters to communicate with my volunteers and audience members. Revise them to fit the needs for your program.

THE PLAYBILL

I used a word processing program to create the playbill for our Lenten Service at my school during the third and fourth production. I printed it up on an 8 ½"X 11" white sheet of paper and then used a copy machine to mass produce the playbill. I copied it onto pastel purple paper for my audience members (purple is a Lenten color in the Catholic Church). Set up your page as landscape view. Then, using the formatting options, separate it into three columns so that you are able to fold it into three parts.

The following pages show how I separated the program's schedule into three columns so that it turned out the correct way as it was folded into three sections, like a pamphlet. This written piece of work has U.S. copyright protection, so please be respectful by indicating the author of the play, Heather Cleaver, and the editor, Otilia Nigaglioni. I know that this document may look backwards, but trust me, if you include these things on the columns as it is shown, your playbill will turn out perfectly when you copy it on a double-sided page. Experiment with font types and sizes to make the schedule of your program fit onto the correct columns of the page. Insert clip art or symbols, such as a crucifix, musical notes, etc. to make your playbill visually appealing.

Print the two sides on white paper, and then reproduce as many double-sided copies as you need on a copy machine using your color choice of copy paper. If you wish to include different songs or prayers in your prayer service, double check your printed copy to make sure everything is in the correct order on your white master copy pages. Place the sheets against each other as if this was your double-sided copy, and then fold them into three sections. You may need to experiment several times to order the layout perfectly, but it will look awesome when it is finished!

_____ (Name of Institution presenting the play)

Lenten Prayer Service

A Children's Play of The Stations of the Cross
An Adaptation from the Holy Bible

(insert clip art here, such as a crucifix)

Written by Heather Cleaver
Edited by Otilia Nigaglioni
Produced and Directed
by _____
Presented by _____

Thank you to all the parents who have practiced and worked hard with their children to make this play possible. It would not have been successful without you.
The teachers are also grateful to the wonderful and awesome students who put together a great production.

Thank you all for joining us to reflect on the difficult journey of Jesus.
We hope you enjoyed our prayer service. May it remind you of all that Jesus has done for you.
We wish you a
Happy and Blessed Easter.
Enjoy your break!

Cast of Characters:

Jesus: _____
Mary: _____
Simon: _____
Veronica: _____
Weeping Women and children: _____
Pontius Pilate: _____
Soldiers: _____

Angry Crowd: _____

Narrators:

_____
_____
_____

Opening Song:
Hosea (Come Back to Me) -by Gregory Norbert
Led by _____

(Include page number)

Gospel Reading:
John: 14:1-4 or John 17:1-17
Read by _____

Follow Jesus' path as we act out
A Children's Play of The Stations of the Cross –Written by Heather Cleaver
-Edited by Otilia Nigaglioni

Performed by the _____ (name of group)

I Jesus is Condemned to Death
II Jesus Takes Up His Cross
III Jesus Falls the First Time
IV Jesus Meets His Mother, Mary
V Simon Helps Jesus Carry His Cross
VI Veronica Wipes Jesus' Face
VII Jesus Falls the Second Time
VIII Jesus Meets the Weeping Women and Children
IX Jesus Falls the Third Time
X Jesus is Stripped of His Garments
XI Jesus is Nailed to the Cross
XII Jesus Dies on the Cross
XIII Jesus is Taken Down from the Cross
XIV Jesus is Laid in the Tomb
(Reflection Song:
Jesus, Remember Me, When You Come into Your Kingdom -by Taizé.)
XV Jesus Rises from the Dead

Closing Prayer:
All: Our Father

Closing Song:
Were You There When They Crucified My Lord? –Author unknown, traditional Negro Spiritual song
Led by _____

Verse 1: Were you there when they crucified my Lord? (2X's)

Refrain: Oh, sometimes it causes me to tremble, tremble, tremble. (Repeat verse again. Then, sing the next verse.)

Verse 2: Were you there when they nailed him to the tree? (2X's)

Verse 3: Were you there when they laid him in the tomb? (2X's)

Verse 4: Were you there when God raised him from the tomb? (2X's)

SAMPLE LETTER REQUESTING DONATED MATERIALS

(Send to parents, volunteers, or community helpers.)

Date

Dear _____,

_____ (name of acting group) are in the process of putting together ***A Children's Play of the Stations of the Cross*** written by Heather Cleaver. We will perform this on _____ (date) at _____ (time) a.m./p.m.

However, we need some help. We would like to make some of our costumes out of white bed sheets, colored pillow cases, and one blue bed sheet. If you have any of these materials and can spare them, our classes would greatly appreciate them. Please send them to _____ (name of person or name location to send through) as soon as you are able. We will practice with them and use them for the play. You will get your sheets back all in one piece after we use them for our play! An update about this play will be sent home in a letter so that parents, relatives, and friends may attend. Thanks in advance for your generosity.

Sincerely,

_____ (name your students, church, community, or theater)

SAMPLE LETTER FOR DELEGATED SERVICES

(Send out to volunteers, community members, teachers, etc.)

Date

Dear Teachers,

I have given you a copy of the playbill for ***A Children's Play of the Stations of the Cross*** so that you may follow along on _____ (date). I have also enclosed enough copies for each student. Please distribute these pamphlets to your students prior to the play so that they may follow along and participate in singing along.

You may want to prep your students about each Station so that they are not shocked about some of the things Jesus had to suffer. Also, please keep the area between the pillars clear. ***A Children's Play of the Stations of the Cross*** will be performed in the middle of the Auditorium. Have students sit along the sides facing inward.

Thanks,

_____ (your signature and/or printed name)

SAMPLE INVITATION LETTER TO ATTEND THE PLAY

(Send to parents and relatives for a play performed in a school setting. Please revise if you are catering to another audience.)

Date

Dear Parents and Relatives,

You are cordially invited to attend our Lenten Prayer Service for _____ (our school, our church community, etc). This will take place on _____ (date), at _____ (time) a.m./p.m.. If you would like to give a donation for admission, the proceeds will be given to _____ (name of charity or your community) for _____ (cause/reason for fundraising).

We will begin at _____ (time) a.m./p.m.. The entire school and welcomed guests will participate in the prayer service. The prayer service will include songs, readings, prayers, and ***A Children's Play of the Stations of the Cross*** (written by Heather Cleaver), which will be performed by _____ (grade level or name of acting group). We welcome you to join us in reflection about what Jesus went through and how he overcame death through his Resurrection. We have been practicing very hard, and we want to show others what Jesus has done for all of us and for all of you.

Guests are also welcome to stay for _____ (name the event or explain that refreshments will be served if this is what you are planning). Thank you to all who have already donated to _____ (charity, community, or cause). The play will end at approximately _____ (time) a.m./p.m. Students will then be dismissed at _____ (time) a.m./p.m. for Easter Break.

We want to share the Good News about Jesus. Let's celebrate it together. God bless you! We hope to see you there!

Sincerely,

_____ (name your students, church, community, or theater)

VII

MY PICTURES OF
THE STATIONS OF THE CROSS

MY PICTURES OF THE STATIONS OF THE CROSS

Here are some ideas that you may use for your pictures of the Stations of the Cross:

➢ Illustrate your own pictures.

➢ Make this a family project and illustrate pictures together with family members.

➢ Use the internet to find and print up pictures of the Stations of the Cross, and affix them to the pages with glue stick or rubber cement.

➢ Take pictures of your production, and then paste the photos of the different scenes with glue stick or rubber cement. You may want to print up several copies of the photos and share them with the other cast members for their books.

➢ Take pictures of the Stations of the Cross at your church, print up the photos using a colored printer, and affix them to the pages with glue stick or rubber cement.

I   JESUS IS CONDEMNED TO DEATH

II JESUS TAKES UP HIS CROSS

III JESUS FALLS THE FIRST TIME

IV JESUS MEETS HIS MOTHER, MARY

V SIMON HELPS JESUS CARRY HIS CROSS

VI VERONICA WIPES JESUS' FACE

VII JESUS FALLS THE SECOND TIME

VIII   JESUS MEETS THE WEEPING WOMEN AND CHILDREN

IX   JESUS FALLS THE THIRD TIME

X JESUS IS STRIPPED OF HIS GARMENTS

XI JESUS IS NAILED TO THE CROSS

XII JESUS DIES ON THE CROSS

XIII   JESUS IS TAKEN DOWN FROM THE CROSS

XIV JESUS IS LAID IN THE TOMB

XV JESUS RISES FROM THE DEAD

A NOTE TO THE CAST MEMBERS FROM THE AUTHOR

Congratulations to you for making the final cut! You are now cast in a role for a play that I wrote and produced at my very own school with my students. You are awesome!

I hope this play helps your audience members experience a closer relationship with Jesus. My wish is to help spread the Good News about what Jesus has done for us, and you are making it come true by acting this play out for your audience. As you learn about the Stations of the Cross, it will help you to reflect on what Jesus has done for both you and me.

By you taking a part in ***A Children's Play of the Stations of the Cross***, you are helping others to see Jesus' sad, yet beautiful story. He sacrificed Himself so that His Kingdom would flourish. Jesus' example of His sacrifice for all of us helps us to understand how the sacrifices of our time and service to others can show our love for them.

You are helping me to spread the Good News! Thank you for doing this with me. Your special talents are growing each day. Your stage presence is needed and greatly appreciated. Have fun with this experience, and God bless you!

Sincerely,
Mrs. Heather Cleaver